FAITH ON-LINE

NANDY HEULE

CRC Publications
Grand Rapids, Michigan

Acknowledgments

Unless otherwise indicated, the Scripture quotations in this publication are from the Holy Bible, New International Version, © 1973, 1978, 1984, International Bible Society. Used by permission of Zondervan Bible Publishers.

Library of Congress Cataloging-in-Publication Data

Heule, Nandy, 1961-

Faith on-line / Nandy Heule.

p. cm. — (Acts 2 for small groups)

ISBN 1-56212-197-9

1. Bible. N.T. James—Textbooks. I. Title. II. Series.

BS 2785.5.H48 1996

227'.91'007—dc20 96-9288
CIP

10 9 8 7 6 5 4 3 2 1

CONTENTS

INTRODUCTION

Faith On-line is a call to activate our faith, to put it to work, to make it real and alive. That's also the message of the book of James, on which this seven-session course for small groups is based. "Do not merely listen to the word," says James. "Do what it says" (James 1:22).

James, the brother of our Lord and the pastor of the Jerusalem church, wrote his letter to believers who had fled Palestine because of persecution. These were ordinary people who struggled with problems not unlike our own: being patient during suffering, dealing with temptation, favoritism, greed, grumbling, gossip, and arrogance. To all Christians everywhere, pastor James offers warm, practical advice that builds vibrant faith and puts that faith to work in humble action.

Faith On-line is part of the *Acts 2* program for small groups. That program is described in detail below.

WHAT ARE *ACTS 2* SMALL GROUPS?

Acts 2 small groups look and act much like the early church house groups portrayed in Acts 2:42-47. These groups were involved in teaching, fellowship, worship, prayer, enfolding, ministry, social time, and evangelism. All of these features are basic to the life of the church. The more these characteristics define a church's small groups, the more they will also define the larger congregation.

Acts 2 groups consist of three to fifteen people who are committed to meeting regularly together to support each other and explore some aspect of the Christian life. Six important features characterize an effective *Acts 2* small group.

MAJOR FEATURES OF *ACTS 2* SMALL GROUPS

BUILDING CHRISTIAN COMMUNITY

Acts 2 groups are more than study groups; study is only one of several important activities. The basic purpose of an *Acts 2* group is to build Christian community by developing meaningful relationships among group members. All of us long to be loved and cared for in an accepting and supportive environment. A good group fosters a level of trust and safety that makes intimacy possible. A healthy *Acts 2* group will meet relational needs by sharing the realities of life, praying with and for each other, ministering side by side, and having fun together.

FORMATTED MATERIALS

Each *Acts 2* meeting includes five main segments:

- Opening share time
- Bible discovery
- Reflection
- Prayer
- Planning for ministry

Groups that follow this format are likely to succeed. If these five elements are not deliberately built into each meeting, groups may shortchange themselves by inadvertently omitting, for example, silent reflection or ministry planning. The *Acts 2* materials provide a regular format that will ensure coverage of each element in all meetings.

TRAINED LEADERS

Ineffective leadership is the primary cause of failure in small groups. Qualified *Acts 2* leaders are trained, supported, and held accountable for what happens in their group.

A training workshop —"Small Groups that Build Up Christians and Churches"—is available (contact CRC Publications for details). After the training workshop and before starting their own *Acts 2* groups in their local church, leaders should experience an *Acts 2* group. This training teaches them the fundamentals of small group leadership by seeing and by doing.

In addition to training leaders, each church is urged to hold regular meetings for small group leaders. These meetings grant leaders the opportunity to enhance their leadership skills, learn from each other's insights and frustrations, report progress, and support each other. The leaders' group becomes, in essence, a support group for the leaders. Trained, supported small group leaders are much more likely to be effective.

GROWTH AND REPRODUCTION

Not many small groups have an outward focus. Small groups often become ingrown and self-serving, a holy huddle that shuts out the concerns of nonmembers. To break this pattern, a small group must deliberately reach out. We suggest placing an empty chair at all your meetings to remind you of the next person God will bring to the group. Group members can pray for and seek persons to fill that chair. In addition, the group may sponsor or attend social events to identify and connect with potential new members. *Acts 2* groups aspire to grow and reproduce a new daughter group every two to three years.

New additions should always be a group decision. Members need to seek the approval of the whole group before inviting someone. New persons who attend should always start on a trial basis. If they don't fit into the group, they should be encouraged to look for another group where they will be more comfortable.

When *Acts 2* groups form new groups, the leader selects two or three members, including an apprentice leader, to be the core of the new group. The group then commissions them to form the new group and sends them off with a blessing. If other members of the group want to join this new group, they are free to do so, if invited.

MINISTRY ORIENTATION

A small group of people who study the Bible are in a good position to begin doing what it says. *Acts 2* groups do ministry as well as talk about it.

All members should be active in one or more of the tasks needed to maintain the group:

- Leader
- Assistant or apprentice leader
- Host or hostess
- Prayer leader
- Service project coordinator
- Outreach facilitator or social activity coordinator

In addition, all are encouraged to pray for persons who might join the group or for those who simply need prayers. All members are also encouraged to become involved in planned group service projects.

LEADER-RECRUITED GROUPS

Assigning people to groups may be the simplest and easiest way to start a cluster of small groups, but training several leaders and sending them to find their own group members is usually more effective. When a few of the invitees have accepted, the leader seeks their input in further choices. The group grows gradually as potential members respond to specific invitations. Groups that form this way are much more likely to bond, since they have chosen each other. They will also continue inviting others.

A church using this approach is likely to have a higher percentage of people involved in small groups than those using other methods. First, people sometimes say no to small groups because they fear being placed with people they don't like. The personal leader-recruiting system gives them more control over those with whom they will be grouped. Second, many people who will not respond to a public solicitation will respond to a personal invitation; this is especially true if the invitation comes from someone they know.

COORDINATED BY A DIRECTOR

Every local church with a small group program should have a director or coordinator of small groups. The director should schedule and lead regular leaders' meetings. He or she will receive reports from the leaders and hold them accountable to the goals that they have set. The director should also visit each of the small groups two or three times a year and give the leader an outsider's perspective on the group.

The director, as servant-leader, should build a relationship with each small group leader or leader couple in order to extend the needed support and encouragement. He or she should be available to assist them in formulating goals and plans, identifying and recruiting apprentice leaders, and finding new members. The director should also be familiar with the church's greeting and welcoming systems and be able to channel the names of church visitors to small group leaders.

WHAT HAPPENS IN AN *ACTS 2* GROUP?

One *Acts 2* small group I attended went like this. Guests began arriving about ten minutes early for the 7:00 meeting. On their way to the family room, they helped themselves to beverages and snacks set out by the hostess. Every person who arrived was greeted cordially, and we chatted about everyday things.

At about 7:05, the leader started the meeting, although everyone had not yet arrived. He asked a group member to read the first of the opening share questions. Responses were lively and numerous.

Another couple arrived and was welcomed by the group. For their benefit, the leader explained where we were in the session. The group continued sharing, moving on to the second (and more personal) of the sharing questions.

Our leader explained that some of the things we had been talking about were also addressed in today's Bible study. Someone read the opening comments and the Scripture passage. The leader read the first question and invited responses. We spent about twenty-five minutes digging into the Bible passages, using the discovery questions provided and asking some of our own questions. Twice our leader referred us to the Helpful Notes provided in the lesson. The study ended with the leader's summary of the main ideas.

A brief reflection time came next. Everyone worked individually and in silence as we wrote our personal responses to the four reflection questions. We had a chance to think about our personal relationship with God and to prepare for the question that preceded the prayer time: "How do I want the group to pray for me?"

Before we prayed together, most of us shared some joys and concerns. We mentioned needs in the lives of hurting persons we knew. Though some of us were a bit nervous about the prayer time, the leader put us at ease by starting us out with one-word prayers of praise. He began with "Father God, we praise you for . . . ," and we completed the sentence by naming a dozen or more qualities of God. Next came "Father, we thank you for . . . ," and we finished the sentence with short expressions of gratitude. Finally we said one- or two-sentence prayers of intercession. Someone remembered to pray for the person who would fill our empty chair. This was a comfortable and stimulating time.

The last thing we did was plan for ministry. We started by identifying three unchurched persons who would be on our prayer list. We added two singles who were fringe members of our church and a young couple who were just beginning to attend. We agreed that each of us would pray for each listed person a couple of times each week.

We made no progress on planning a social event, but we did decide to ask the pastor for a list of those attending the church's new member class. We also chose to take on one service project during the year. One couple agreed to lead this.

After the formal meeting, we took more refreshments and continued to visit with each other. Some group members left almost immediately. Two couples lingered for another half hour.

FUNDAMENTALS OF SMALL GROUP LIFE

FIVE BASIC FUNCTIONS

A good group will ordinarily include

A social/recreational time. Fun time is a natural and important part of the life of the group. Activities apart from the regular meetings develop stronger group relationships and especially benefit the children of the families involved.

Life-application Bible study. The questions in the Bible study section of each lesson will help you discover what the Bible says. The application element is particularly important. People tend to lose interest in abstract discussions that do not relate to their lives.

Meaningful prayer time. Everyone should have a chance to share joys and concerns and contribute to the prayer time. Not everyone is expected to pray out loud, but everyone should be allowed to do so. Don't be afraid of periods of silence—during these times, individuals may pray silently or simply bow before God in silence. The prayer time may also be a time for worship—simply focusing on God and rejoicing in his goodness.

Regular sharing opportunities. The Christian life is meant to be a shared life. The New Testament emphasizes that Christians come to know each other well enough to bear each other's burdens, teach and admonish one another, and even confess faults to each other. This will happen best in a small group if members are free to share with the group what life is really like for them. Of course, what is shared *must* be kept confidential.

Ministry opportunities. Every believer has at least one spiritual gift. A small group is a wonderful place to use that gift and to find support. Don't let your small group become another sit-and-soak experience—the church already has enough of those.

GROUP PATTERNS

The best place for a group to meet is in a familiar, informal setting. Around a kitchen table or a family room is ideal. Groups that meet weekly will have the most impact, but meeting weekly may not be realistic. Most groups meet biweekly or twice a month. Groups that meet less frequently lose the continuity necessary for building relationships. Biweekly meetings can be a little longer than weekly meetings but should be kept under two hours.

Each group should set growth and ministry activity goals and keep a record of its progress in meeting the set goals. Some things simply will not happen unless plans are laid and progress is regularly reviewed. Groups should try to spin off a new small group every two to three years. (See Group Goals Planning Sheet on page 57.)

LEADERSHIP RESPONSIBILITY

The leader's primary responsibility is to organize and lead the regular small group meeting. This means involving people in sharing, prayer, and Bible study and working to keep a healthy balance between these various elements. A good balance of available time is as follows:

- About 25% on sharing. *Acts 2* material suggests sharing before the Bible study and before the prayer time.
- About 25% on prayer. Initially you will probably not spend this much time in prayer; as the group members come to know each other, however, this time will likely increase.
- About 40% on Bible study.
- About 10% on ministry planning.

Use the notes in the margin addressed to the leader as helps to involve members in the various activities.

Between meetings, leaders should pray regularly for group members and continue contact with group members. Pastoral care is the responsibility of the whole group, but the leader must see that it is done.

Every leader should also identify an apprentice leader. This person can assist in leadership functions and prepare to lead a new, spin-off group.

Leaders should spend several hours preparing for each meeting. Be thoroughly familiar with the main theme, the Bible passages, and the directions in the material. Prepare for each question (for some, perhaps you'd rather substitute your own questions). Highlight key phrases or words for easy reference during the meeting. Develop extra questions that can help the group probe an area that needs attention. Prepare your heart as well as your thoughts. Above all, blanket the group and the time you will spend together with prayer, asking God to direct and protect you and to make himself known through his Word and Spirit.

COMMON PROBLEMS TO AVOID

Following are problems common to small groups. Any can severely diminish the effectiveness of a group or even kill it.

Shallow relationships. Sharing our ideas but not ourselves, praying for others while hiding our own pain, applying the Bible truths generally but avoiding specific personal application—these behaviors will yield shallow relationships. An increasing amount of honesty and openness are necessary in order to develop deep and meaningful relationships.

Overly intellectual discussions. Dealing only with the intellectual dimensions hinders spiritual growth and the development of Christian community. Try to spend at least half of your group study time relating biblical truths to our daily lives.

Unused gifts. A small group is a perfect place to identify, confirm, and use spiritual gifts. Groups in which one or two persons take charge do not promote gift development. Leaders are encouraged to share responsibility so that everyone is involved and challenged to use his or her gifts.

Problem members. Compulsive talkers, tangent-chasers, judgmental persons, pity-seekers, or domineering individuals can ruin a group. For the good of the group, leaders must deal with problem members lovingly but firmly.

Lack of confidentiality. Few things will shut down personal sharing faster than breaches of confidentiality. Be sure to regularly review the ground rules for preserving confidentiality and deal quickly with any compromise of these standards.

Little meaningful prayer. Perfunctory or impersonal prayers, quick opening and closing prayers, and prayers that do not touch our real lives will stultify a group. Prayer is one place where people can really connect with each other.

Holy huddles. Groups who focus inwardly soon become cliques or "holy huddles." An intimate, close-knit group is not a clique as long as it looks to the interests of others as well as its own. An exclusive small group that shuts out the cares and concerns of others has a problem.

GETTING STARTED

After appropriate training, leaders list people whom they would like to have in their group. The list should include twice the number needed, since only half of those invited are likely to accept.

The next step is to prioritize the list and extend invitations to those on top of the list. Give invitations with full explanation; ask people simply to try the group. Their decision to join is not final until they have experienced at least two meetings. Those who accept the initial invitation may help choose additional group members.

When six to eight persons have accepted the initial invitation, set a date, time, and place for the first meeting. I suggest making the first meeting a social evening at which people get acquainted and are informed about the purpose and format of the group. They may also be asked at this time what they would like to study. Be prepared, however, to make a suggestion rather than to leave it wide open. Most new groups will welcome the leader's recommendation of material to be used. Give them plenty of time to ask questions too.

VALUE TO THE CHURCH

Small groups are of great value to the church. They provide a good place to grow. They're like greenhouses, shutting out the cold and letting in the light necessary for growth.

Small groups also decentralize caregiving. Small group members who know each other's needs and have regular contact can minister to each other in a way that diminishes the need for attention by paid staff.

Furthermore, small groups break a natural path for evangelism, assimilation, and discipleship. Relationships draw people to Christ, bring them into the church, and help them mature. Relationships are the primary strength of the small group.

Starting and maintaining a good small group program is not a quick and easy task. It requires gifted people, solid training, and constant administrative attention. Above all, it requires the grace and power of God released through prayer.

Acts 2 groups reflect the realities of the Acts 2:42-47 experience, in which early Christians "devoted themselves to the apostles' teaching and to fellowship, to the breaking of bread and to prayer," and in which "believers had everything in common ... gave to anyone as he had need ... ate together with glad and sincere hearts ... and added to their number daily."

Alvin J. Vander Griend
Minister of Evangelism Resources
Christian Reformed Church Home Missions

Session 1

HANDLING HARD TIMES

OPENING SHARE TIME

10-15 minutes

Sharing is an important function of *Acts 2* small groups. Your relationships with others in the group will deepen as you share openly with others and maintain confidentiality. Notice that the first Share Time question is usually general and the second is more specific and personal.

1. What are several of the main difficulties or trials that the church of Jesus Christ faces today?

2. James writes to Christians who were "facing trials of many kinds." If you wish, please share one recent "trial" that you personally have experienced.

Leader: Distribute books and welcome everyone to this study of the book of James. Use the two Share Time questions to introduce today's theme: handling hard times. When discussing question 2, be prepared to begin with your own response.

BIBLE DISCOVERY TIME

20-30 minutes

Read James 1:1-12. James writes to Jewish believers who have been "scattered among the nations" because of persecution and who now face "trials of many kinds." What should our attitude be when we, as modern Christians, face our own inevitable trials and troubles? James offers what may seem like strange advice.

Ask one or two group members to read the introductory comments and the Bible passage. Lead the group in discussing the questions that follow the passage.

> *[1]James, a servant of God and of the Lord Jesus Christ,*
> *To the twelve tribes scattered among the nations:*
> *Greetings.*
>
> *[2]Consider it pure joy, my brothers, whenever you face*
> *trials of many kinds, [3]because you know that the test-*
> *ing of your faith develops perseverance. [4]Perseverance*
> *must finish its work so that you may be mature and*
> *complete, not lacking anything. [5]If any of you lacks*
> *wisdom, he should ask God, who gives generously to*
> *all without finding fault, and it will be given to him.*
> *[6]But when he asks, he must believe and not doubt,*
> *because he who doubts is like a wave of the sea,*
> *blown and tossed by the wind. [7]That man should not*
> *think he will receive anything from the Lord; [8]he is a*
> *double-minded man, unstable in all he does.*

9 The brother in humble circumstances ought to take pride in his high position. 10 But the one who is rich should take pride in his low position, because he will pass away like a wild flower. 11 For the sun rises with scorching heat and withers the plant; its blossom falls and its beauty is destroyed. In the same way, the rich man will fade away even while he goes about his business.

12 Blessed is the man who perseveres under trial, because when he has stood the test, he will receive the crown of life that God has promised to those who love him.

Leader: To provide some general information on the book of James and some background on verses 1-12, ask someone to read Helpful Notes aloud. For more background on James, see the introduction to *The NIV Study Bible*.

Helpful Notes

- *James, a servant of God and of the Lord Jesus Christ.* James was most likely a brother of Jesus. Initially James did not believe; later he accepted Christ and became the head of the church in Jerusalem.
- *To the twelve tribes scattered among the nations.* James wrote to Jewish Christians who were driven from Palestine by persecution to places as far away as Phoenicia, Cyprus, and Syrian Antioch. James probably wrote his letter around 43-44 A.D., after Stephen's execution but before Paul's missionary journeys. The main theme of his letter: knowing the faith is not enough—it must be put into practice.
- *Trials of many kinds.* Trials, testing, and temptations are all the same word in Greek, the language that James used to write this letter. The Jewish Christians to whom James wrote knew all about trials. Driven from their homeland and exploited by local landowners in alien nations, they desperately needed to cling to their faith.

Be sure to include James 1:12 in your discussion of question 1. You may also want the group to read Matthew 5:11-12 and Romans 5:3-5.

1. How can it be "pure joy" to suffer "trials of many kinds"? Must we somehow "enjoy" the suffering we experience? What do you make of James's strange-sounding advice?

For additional passages about wisdom, refer the group to Proverbs 1:7; 31:25-26, 30; Psalm 111:10; Luke 2:40, 52.

2. James says that God will give wisdom to all who sincerely ask for it. Have you thought about asking God for wisdom lately (v. 5)? What would you expect to receive if God gave you wisdom?
3. Believers in humble circumstances can take pride in what kind of "high position" (v. 9)? The rich can take

pride in what kind of "low position" (vv. 10-11)? Upon what does the ultimate standing of rich *and* poor depend?

4. Has God used a time of trial and difficulty to help you mature in your faith or to gain in wisdom? If you wish, tell the group about such an experience. You may want to refer back to something you mentioned during Opening Share Time.

Read James 1:13-18. Does God send trials and difficulties into our lives? May we blame God for our troubles? Satan? Who is our real enemy? These are some of the questions James answers in these verses.

Leader: Continue your Bible study by reading the introductory comments and discussing the questions.

> 13*When tempted, no one should say, "God is tempting
> me." For God cannot be tempted by evil, nor does he
> tempt anyone;* 14*but each one is tempted when, by
> his own evil desire, he is dragged away and enticed.*
> 15*Then, after desire has conceived, it gives birth to sin;
> and sin, when it is full-grown, gives birth to death.*
>
> 16*Don't be deceived, my dear brothers.* 17*Every good
> and perfect gift is from above, coming down from the
> Father of the heavenly lights, who does not change
> like shifting shadows.* 18*He chose to give us birth
> through the word of truth, that we might be a kind of
> firstfruits of all he created.*

Helpful Notes

- *Firstfruits of all he created.* This could refer to the early believers being the first of what would eventually be a huge "crop" of reborn people. Or, more generally, it could mean that God intends all believers to be like the choicest, best part of the harvest.

1. James says that God does not tempt us. What do we mean, then, when we pray, "Lead us not into temptation"? What is God's role in temptation?
2. Where do our bitter thoughts and evil desires come from, if not from God? May we rightly blame Satan? If not, then who or what may we blame?
3. What do verses 16-18 tell us about God? How does God help us in our struggles, trials, and temptations?

When discussing question 2, refer to James 4:7 as well as James 1:13-15.

MAIN IDEAS

Leader: Ask someone to read Main Ideas and Good News. Give the group an opportunity to react to the statements and to add any statements they feel are needed.

- As followers of Christ, we can expect to endure trials and temptations from without and within.
- Such trials and temptations do not come from God, nor are we called to enjoy them. Our task is to accept them, and then by God's grace to persevere and to grow in our faith.
- God always remains on our side in our conflict with evil. He may allow us to face trials, as a commander sends the troops into battle. But he never changes sides to become our enemy.
- God has chosen us to be his children, his "firstfruits." If we persevere, we will be blessed and receive the crown of life (James 1:12).

GOOD NEWS

Our heavenly Father gives us faith, wisdom, and every good and perfect gift to help us in our struggle against evil. By God's grace, we can persevere and receive the crown of life!

REFLECTION TIME

7-10 minutes

Group members work individually during Reflection Time. Jot down your own personal responses to reflection questions. You may want to point out that Reflection Time and Prayer Time often include praise or thanksgiving, confession, requests or petitions for ourselves, and intercession for others.

Jot down your personal reflections, using the questions below.

1. What "good gifts" have I received recently for which I can thank and praise God?

2. Does anything I learned during today's session prompt me to ask God's forgiveness?

3. Is there someone I know who is enduring a time of trial or difficulty? How can we as a group pray for that person today?

4. Do I need wisdom and strength to deal with a trial or struggle in my own life? Is this something the group can pray about?

PRAYER TIME

PREPARATION

5-10 minutes

As you are comfortable, share any answers or parts of answers from questions 1-4. Share especially those insights that will help the group pray meaningfully with you and for you.

Leader: Go around the circle, giving each person an opportunity to share his or her response to one or two of the reflection questions. Encourage members to mention ways that you as a group can pray for them.

PRAYER

10-15 minutes

Read these guidelines aloud before the prayer time begins. Initially you may spend considerably less than the allotted time in prayer, but as the group grows closer, the prayer time should expand.

Begin with prayers of thanks or praise for the gifts that God has given us.

Continue by praying for any needs mentioned earlier. Pray especially for wisdom and strength when facing trials and temptations.

Feel free to contribute more than once.

Expect some times of silence. Use them to listen to the Spirit or to offer a silent prayer.

Close the prayer time by reading this prayer in unison:

[Lord],

Lead us not into temptation
but deliver us from the evil one. . . .

Leader: You may want to inform the group that the closing prayers suggested in this course come from the Heidelberg Catechism's explanation of the petitions of the Lord's Prayer. These explanations are stated as prayers themselves. We suggest saying them in unison to end your prayer time.

By ourselves we are too weak
to hold our own even for a moment.

And our sworn enemies—
the devil, the world, and our own flesh—
never stop attacking us.

And so, Lord,
uphold us and make us strong
with the strength of your Holy Spirit,
so that we may not go down to defeat
in this spiritual struggle,
but may firmly resist our enemies
until we finally win the complete victory. Amen.

—Answer 127 of the Heidelberg Catechism

PLANNING FOR MINISTRY

Refer the group to Appendix A: Group Goals Planning Sheet.

Service or ministry is an important function of *Acts 2* small groups. This section will suggest some ways that your group can plan for ministry.

If your group is meeting for the first time, you'll want to establish some goals for your meetings. Discuss each goal and consider its value to your group and your church before you set the goal. Be sure the goals are something you can accomplish.

If your group has been meeting for some time, review the group's goals and make any necessary revisions or additions.

Session 2

DOING THE WORD

OPENING SHARE TIME

10-15 minutes

Today's opening questions should start you thinking about James's main message: "Just do it!"

1. Remember back when your teacher or parent told you to do something simply because "I said so. Period"? Have you caught yourself saying something like this to your child? Share and smile.
2. In today's passage James tells us to just "do what it [God's Word] says." Period. How do you (honestly!) react to such an order? Why?

Leader: As you go around the circle sharing responses, persons who choose not to share may simply say pass. Tell group members that this is always an acceptable response.

BIBLE DISCOVERY TIME

20-30 minutes

Read James 1:19-27. If we are indeed the "firstfruits of all [God] created" (James 1:18), then we should definitely act that way. In this section, James begins to spell out what that means.

> [19]*My dear brothers, take note of this: Everyone should be quick to listen, slow to speak and slow to become angry, [20]for man's anger does not bring about the righteous life that God desires. [21]Therefore, get rid of all moral filth and the evil that is so prevalent and humbly accept the word planted in you, which can save you.*
>
> [22]*Do not merely listen to the word, and so deceive yourselves. Do what it says. [23]Anyone who listens to the word but does not do what it says is like a man who looks at his face in a mirror [24]and, after looking at himself, goes away and immediately forgets what he looks like. [25]But the man who looks intently into the perfect law that gives freedom, and continues to do this, not forgetting what he has heard, but doing it—he will be blessed in what he does.*
>
> [26]*If anyone considers himself religious and yet does not keep a tight rein on his tongue, he deceives him-*

Ask someone to read the introductory comments. Have someone else read the Bible passage. Lead the group in discussing the questions that follow the passage.

self and his religion is worthless. [27]*Religion that God our Father accepts as pure and faultless is this: to look after orphans and widows in their distress and to keep oneself from being polluted by the world.*

Leader: Refer to Helpful Notes when they pertain to your discussion. A group member may read them aloud.

Helpful Notes

- *Immediately forgets what he looks like.* This refers to a meaningless experience, one without lasting effects—similar to listening to God's Word without doing what it says.
- *Considers himself religious.* We cannot be truly religious (pious) if our devotion to God does not show in the way we speak to each other.
- *Orphans and widows.* Without social services, welfare plans, or pensions, these children of God would be defenseless, unprotected, and living in grinding poverty.

Don't feel you must discuss every question. Try to stay within your time limits for each section. When discussing question 3, you may want to read the parable of the wise and foolish builders (Matt. 7:24-27).

1. What does it mean to be "quick to listen"? Is it easier to listen well to the people we love the most? Or is it easier to listen well to outsiders? Why?
2. James urges believers to be "quick to listen, slow to speak and slow to become angry." Of this trio, which is most difficult for you personally? Why?
3. Why do you think James is so concerned about "keeping a tight rein" on what we say? Don't our actions speak louder than our words?
4. What things contribute to our merely hearing the Word of God but not doing it? What kind of blessings come to us when we do what God tells us to do in his Word?

Read James 2:1-13. In this section of his letter, James hits his readers with a stinging and close-to-home example of "being polluted by the world."

> [1]*My brothers, as believers in our glorious Lord Jesus Christ, don't show favoritism.* [2]*Suppose a man comes into your meeting wearing a gold ring and fine clothes, and a poor man in shabby clothes also comes in.* [3]*If you show special attention to the man wearing fine clothes and say, "Here's a good seat for you," but say to the poor man, "You stand there" or "Sit on the floor by my feet,"* [4]*have you not discriminated among yourselves and become judges with evil thoughts?*

[5]Listen, my dear brothers: Has not God chosen those who are poor in the eyes of the world to be rich in faith and to inherit the kingdom he promised those who love him? [6]But you have insulted the poor. Is it not the rich who are exploiting you? Are they not the ones who are dragging you into court? [7]Are they not the ones who are slandering the noble name of him to whom you belong?

[8]If you really keep the royal law found in Scripture, "Love your neighbor as yourself," you are doing right. [9]But if you show favoritism, you sin and are convicted by the law as lawbreakers. [10]For whoever keeps the whole law and yet stumbles at just one point is guilty of breaking all of it.

[11]For he who said, "Do not commit adultery," also said, "Do not murder." If you do not commit adultery but do commit murder, you have become a lawbreaker.

[12]Speak and act as those who are going to be judged by the law that gives freedom, [13]because judgment without mercy will be shown to anyone who has not been merciful. Mercy triumphs over judgment!

Helpful Notes

- *Your meeting.* Probably refers to a place of Christian worship, as distinguished from the Jewish synagogue.
- *Judged by the law that gives freedom.* God's standard is not the burdensome, fussy edicts of the prescribed religious practices of the day; rather, it is the liberating will of God, whose heart is concerned for the weakest of his children. If we do not share that concern, James says, God will not be merciful to us.

1. How does money "talk" in our secular society today? Do the opinions of wealthier church members carry more weight than those of others in our church communities?

2. Showing favoritism to the wealthy may seem like a minor issue to some believers. Why, according to James, is this definitely not the case?

3. As believers, what should be our motivation for "showing mercy" to the poor and oppressed in our society?

Leader: Ask someone to read Main Ideas and Good News. Give the group an opportunity to react to the statements and to add any statements they feel are needed.

MAIN IDEAS

- We should be "quick to listen, slow to speak, and slow to become angry." Our speech should be Christlike.
- It's not enough just to listen to God's Word; we also need to do what it says.
- If we are truly religious, we'll help the helpless and show no favoritism toward the rich at the expense of the poor.
- In our own lives, we have seen God's mercy triumphing over his judgment. Therefore we should show mercy to others, as we attempt to live by God's liberating "law of love."

GOOD NEWS

When we do what God wants us to do, we will be truly free, and God will give us his blessing.

REFLECTION TIME

7-10 minutes

Group members work individually during Reflection Time. Jot down your own personal responses to reflection questions.

Jot down your personal reflections, using the questions below.

1. What did I learn today for which I can thank and praise God? Is there some special mercy God has recently shown me for which I should give thanks?

2. Have I in any way insulted the poor? Do I need to ask forgiveness for showing favoritism in church, at home, or on the job?

3. Do I know someone who is suffering financial pressures or economic insecurities? If so, how can the group pray for him or her today?

PRAYER TIME

PREPARATION

5-10 minutes

As you are comfortable, share any answers or parts of answers from questions 1-3. If you have additional prayer requests for yourself or others, please share these at this time.

Leader: Go around the circle, giving each person an opportunity to share his or her response to one or two of the reflection questions. As always, assume that confidentiality will apply to all responses.

PRAYER

10-15 minutes

Begin with expressions of thanks and praise for the mercy God has shown to us. The group may want to sing a favorite praise song or two as part of this time.

Ask a group member to read these guidelines aloud before the prayer time begins.

Continue by praying for any needs mentioned earlier. In your prayers, try to be quick to listen and slow to speak. Don't worry about what you're going to say or what anybody else might pray or not pray.

Close the prayer time by reading this prayer in unison:

[Lord],
Forgive us our debts
as we also have forgiven our debtors. . . .

Because of Christ's blood,
do not hold against us, poor sinners that we are,
any of the sins we do
or the evil that constantly clings to us.

Forgive us just as we are fully determined,
as evidence of your grace in us,
to forgive our neighbors. Amen.

—Answer 126 of the Heidelberg Catechism

PLANNING FOR MINISTRY

Leader: You may want to suggest a few possible service projects for your group's consideration. Welcome ideas from group members as well.

Especially appropriate this week are deeds of loving service to others. Perhaps your group is already involved in some aspect of serving your community or congregation. If not, you may want to discuss taking on a service project. What could your group do that would truly serve persons in need? What could your group do that would fit the gifts, schedules, and resources of group members? When could you do this? Who will take the lead?

In your prayers at home this week, be especially mindful of a person or cause you know that is in need. Ask the Spirit to show you how you can genuinely serve such a person or cause.

Session 3

PUTTING OUR FAITH TO WORK

OPENING SHARE TIME

10-15 minutes

Sharing is an important part of these sessions. Notice that both of today's Share Time questions are somewhat personal. We hope such questions help your group grow closer.

1. At one time or another, most of us fail to back up our words with actions (ask your spouse or child or coworker!). Share an example of this from your personal experience, if you wish.

2. Describe a time when you were able to put your faith into action by serving someone or a cause in some way. Why did you do this? Did you receive any unexpected benefits from this service? Did it strengthen your faith in any way?

Leader: Welcome everybody back, then open your discussion with one or both of the questions below. For question 2, assure group members that responding will not indicate they're "bragging" about their service! It's OK to talk about the blessings received from a God-given opportunity to serve others.

If you prefer an alternative question, ask the group to share stories of times when they were the recipients of someone else's "faith in action." When were they blessed by the good deed of a fellow Christian?

BIBLE DISCOVERY TIME

20-30 minutes

Read James 2:14-19. In today's passage, James continues the theme he has summarized in 2:12: "Speak and act as those who are going to be judged by the law that gives freedom." True faith propels believers into action!

As usual, have someone read the introduction and the Bible passage aloud. Then discuss as many of the questions as you wish.

> [14]*What good is it, my brothers, if a man claims to*
> *have faith but has no deeds? Can such faith save*
> *him?* [15]*Suppose a brother or sister is without clothes*
> *and daily food.* [16]*If one of you says to him, "Go, I wish*
> *you well; keep warm and well fed," but does nothing*
> *about his physical needs, what good is it?* [17]*In the*
> *same way, faith by itself, if it is not accompanied by*
> *action, is dead.*
>
> [18]*But someone will say, "You have faith; I have deeds."*
>
> *Show me your faith without deeds, and I will show*
> *you my faith by what I do.* [19]*You believe that there is*

one God. Good! Even the demons believe that—and shudder.

Leader: Refer to Helpful Notes when they pertain to your discussion. A group member may read them aloud.

Helpful Notes

- *What good is it . . . Can such faith save him?* In the original Greek, the grammatical structure expects a resounding no.
- *Go . . . keep warm and well fed.* In the original Greek, this is not a pious wish or a well-meant goodbye. "Well fed" is a vulgarism for "gorge yourself." So this Christian adds insult to injury by telling the hungry, poorly-clothed person: "Go get toasty warm and pig out!"
- *"You have faith; I have deeds." Show me your faith without deeds.* You can't separate faith and works, James says. It's impossible to show someone your faith without deeds—you can only show someone your faith by what you do.

1. Believers do good deeds. They give of themselves. And, according to theologian Lewis Smedes, giving a true gift usually involves an element of risk or sacrifice from the giver. What are some examples of risk or sacrifice that true giving involves?

To put these questions in some context, you may want to read and discuss Matthew 25:14-30 (or invite members to do so at home). Before beginning your discussion, check the time. You are approximately one-third of the way through the session at this time.

2. Do you think it's more or less difficult for those well-endowed with money, talent, and time to do good deeds? Why?
3. Does the need to do good works extend to all believers, including children, elderly, poor, and people with disabilities? Are some of us expected to do more than others?
4. Do you ever dream of doing a good deed that—for you—would be a major step in the "show me your faith by your deeds" category? As you are comfortable, share your "dream" with others. Do you think it is good to have such dreams? What does it take to get us to put our dreams into action?
5. "You believe that there is one God. Good! Even the demons believe that—and shudder!" What point is James making here? In our tradition, have we placed too much emphasis on knowledge, as opposed to deeds?

Ask someone to read the introductory comments and the Scripture passage. The Helpful Notes on this passage make an important point that should also be read aloud.

Read James 2:20-26. James reinforces his argument that faith without works is dead. He cites two examples from Israel's history: Abraham offering his son and Rahab saving the spies.

> [20]*You foolish man, do you want evidence that faith without deeds is useless?* [21]*Was not our ancestor Abraham considered righteous for what he did when he offered his son Isaac on the altar?* [22]*You see that his faith and his actions were working together, and his faith was made complete by what he did.* [23]*And the scripture was fulfilled that says, "Abraham believed God, and it was credited to him as righteousness," and he was called God's friend.* [24]*You see that a person is justified by what he does and not by faith alone.*
>
> [25]*In the same way, was not even Rahab the prostitute considered righteous for what she did when she gave lodging to the spies and sent them off in a different direction?* [26]*As the body without the spirit is dead, so faith without deeds is dead.*
>
> ***Helpful Notes***
>
> - *Justified by what he does and not by faith alone.* This seems to contradict Paul's teaching that we are saved "by grace . . . through faith" (Eph. 2:8). Paul argues that our works can never be good enough to save us. Only Christ can make things right for us with God. James doesn't disagree with this; rather, he *adds* the idea that our knowledge of God's amazing grace will produce good works in us. When we are a new creation in Christ (2 Cor. 5:17), we will by definition engage in good works. We can't help it, says James.

1. Many nonbelievers do acts of great kindness and generosity; however, faith and good deeds work together (cooperate) in believers. What difference, if any, does this make to God? To the doer? To the recipient?

2. Even though Rahab was a prostitute and even though her good deeds had some strings attached (see Joshua 2:12-14), James says she was considered righteous for what she did. How can someone be a prostitute and still be considered righteous? Why do you think James cites her instead of one of the other numerous heroes of faith listed in Hebrews 11?

Leader: Ask someone to read Main Ideas and Good News. Be open to additional ideas that group members offer. You may want to add this comment of John Calvin's to Main Ideas: "Faith alone justifies; but the faith which justifies is not alone.

MAIN IDEAS

- Good deeds alone cannot save us. Faith in Jesus Christ is required.
- But faith alone isn't enough either. Faith and good works must go together. No actions, no faith.
- Knowing about God's grace in our lives—having faith—will compel us to do loving deeds.

GOOD NEWS

"For it is by grace you have been saved, through faith—and this not from yourselves, it is the gift of God—not by works, so that no one can boast. For we are God's workmanship, created in Christ Jesus to do good works, which God prepared in advance for us to do" (Eph. 2:8-10).

REFLECTION TIME

7-10 minutes

Does your meeting place allow all participants enough room to reflect privately? Encourage group members to find a comfortable spot, if possible.

Jot down your personal reflections, using the questions below.

1. I'm saved by grace through faith! Have I thanked God for that recently? Have I thanked him for opportunities to serve in Jesus' name?

2. Can others see that I'm a Christian by what I do? Do I need to confess that I'm long on good intentions but short on good deeds?

3. Can the group pray that I have the courage to undertake a good deed that I've been thinking of doing for a long time?

4. How can the group pray for an economic development worker or missionary who is doing good deeds in Christ's name on our behalf?

PRAYER TIME

PREPARATION

5-10 minutes

As you are comfortable, share any answers or parts of answers from questions 1-4. How would you like the group to pray for you between now and the next time you meet?

Leader: When measured by the standard of good works, all of us fall short. This may be an opportune time to remind the group of God's promise in 1 John 1:8-9.

PRAYER

10-15 minutes

Praise God for every good and perfect gift he gives us (James 1:17).

Ask a group member to read these guidelines aloud before the prayer time begins.

Praise Jesus for taking the ultimate risk and making the ultimate personal sacrifice. By his death he gives us life and frees us to do good.

Pray for the concerns brought up earlier. Pray especially for those who shared their dreams and hopes of putting their faith into action.

Pray for Christians who live their vision by accepting a life of sacrifice and risk in foreign development or missionary work.

Close your prayer time by saying this prayer in unison:

[Lord],

Your will be done on earth as it is in heaven. . . .

Help us and all people
  to reject our own wills
  and to obey your will without any back talk.
  Your will alone is good.

Help us one and all to carry out the work we are called to,

as willingly and faithfully as the angels in heaven. Amen.

—Answer 124 of the Heidelberg Catechism

PLANNING FOR MINISTRY

Leader: Try to be honest together. Participants might not see this particular group as the vehicle for putting their faith into action.

Please continue planning a service project as suggested in session 2.

Session 4

TAMING THE TONGUE

OPENING SHARE TIME

10-15 minutes

"Praise the LORD.

How good it is to sing praises to our God,

how pleasant and fitting to praise him!" (Psalm 147:1).

Our Creator has given us the great gift of human speech. In today's session, we'll look at how we use and misuse this gift.

1. "Words can sometimes, in moments of grace, attain the quality of deeds" (Elie Wiesel). What do you think this means? Can you give an example of when it could be true?
2. Many of us have several favorite hymns that we love to listen to or sing. Mention one of these to the group, along with a few words about why you find this particular song so meaningful.

Leader: If your group approves, how about singing one or more of the songs that group members mention in response to question 2? You could sing now or at the end of the session.

For an alternate opening question, ask, "What's the best way for you personally to praise God? Singing? Worship? Serving? A walk on the beach? Mention a recent time when life seemed good and God seemed near."

BIBLE DISCOVERY TIME

20-30 minutes

Read James 3:1-12. With these verses, James takes a sudden leap back to a topic he introduced at the beginning of his letter (1:19, 26): as believers, we need to be very careful about what we say.

[1]Not many of you should presume to be teachers, my brothers, because you know that we who teach will be judged more strictly. [2]We all stumble in many ways. If anyone is never at fault in what he says, he is a perfect man, able to keep his whole body in check.

[3]When we put bits into the mouths of horses to make them obey us, we can turn the whole animal. [4]Or take ships as an example. Although they are so large and are driven by strong winds, they are steered by a very small rudder wherever the pilot wants to go. [5]Likewise the tongue is a small part of the body, but it makes

Our passage today is short, allowing for a thorough discussion. Take your time responding to the questions. Feel free to ask the group for additional questions they'd like to discuss.

great boasts. Consider what a great forest is set on fire by a small spark. [6]The tongue also is a fire, a world of evil among the parts of the body. It corrupts the whole person, sets the whole course of his life on fire, and is itself set on fire by hell.

[7]All kinds of animals, birds, reptiles and creatures of the sea are being tamed and have been tamed by man, [8]but no man can tame the tongue. It is a restless evil, full of deadly poison.

[9]With the tongue we praise our Lord and Father, and with it we curse men, who have been made in God's likeness. [10]Out of the same mouth come praise and cursing. My brothers, this should not be. [11]Can both fresh water and salt water flow from the same spring? [12]My brothers, can a fig tree bear olives or a grapevine bear figs? Neither can a salt spring produce fresh water.

Helpful Notes

- *We who teach will be judged more strictly.* Here James gives us the only bit of self-disclosure we'll find in the book. He considers himself a teacher, and he knows the risks involved. Those who teach, says James, influence many others; therefore they will be held more accountable.
- *Set on fire by hell.* The devil himself is responsible for the horrible consequences of careless speech. Such speech corrupts the whole person, destroying his or her life. This negative view of speech was prevalent in James's world. He is using well-known metaphors to emphasize his warnings about speech.
- *Made in God's likeness.* By cursing those who reflect God in their very being, we are, in effect, cursing God himself.
- *This should not be.* In the original Greek, the phrase is a strong declaration, somewhat similar to our casual expression "No way!"

Leader: When discussing question 1, you may want to point out that James warns us to keep a tight rein on our tongue or our religion will be worthless (1:26). Since "we all stumble," is he holding us to a standard we can't keep?

1. What does James mean when he says that anyone who controls his speech "is a perfect man, able to keep his whole body in check"? Do you find this observation encouraging or discouraging? Explain.
2. Look back through verses 3-8 and locate the five images James uses to explain the power of speech. Can you add a couple of modern examples to James's

list? Do you typically think of the tongue as setting the course of our lives?

3. In verses 6-7, James hits hard at the way our words can poison, corrupt, and destroy. The tongue is "a restless evil, full of deadly poison," he concludes. Give some examples from history or from your own experience that show the potential for evil that mere words can have.

4. Verses 9 and 10 point out the tongue's potential for praise (as well as cursing). Give an example from history or from your own experience of the positive impact that mere words can have on us.

Leader: When discussing question 4, you may want to refer back to the quote from Elie Wiesel. Encourage group members to talk about times that they were blessed by someone's encouraging or kind words.

5. Verses 9-12 zero in on what must have triggered this extensive warning about the power of speech: James's listeners—who praise God with their fine words—apparently have been "cursing men." James doesn't specify the nature of this "cursing." What forms could it have taken, do you think? What forms might it take in our own congregations today?

6. What point is James making with the three images in verses 11-12?

7. The book of Proverbs is full of practical wisdom about controlling the tongue (see Prov. 10:18-21; 12:18-19; 13:2-3; 15:4; 21:23; 25:15; 26:22-28). Read some or all of these passages, and then talk about how we learn to control our speech, "speaking the truth in love" (Eph. 4:15).

MAIN IDEAS

For a change of pace, have group members sum up the key insights they gained from today's Scripture.

- Our words have a tremendous potential for good or for evil.
- Though true religion demands that we keep our speech under careful control, we all misuse God's gift of speech from time to time.
- God wants our praises, but our religious talk is only impious blather as long as we keep hurting each other with our tongues.
- As we grow in faith and wisdom, we will try to speak the truth in love (Eph. 4:15).

GOOD NEWS

We can praise God with our words! And we know we can be forgiven when we fail to speak the truth in love.

REFLECTION TIME

7-10 minutes

Leader: You may point out that these personal, written reflections can continue to guide your prayers at home.

Jot down your personal reflections, using the questions below.

1. Do I regularly and enthusiastically join God's people in song? Do I praise my God regularly? For what can I thank and praise God today?

2. Have I recently hurt someone by what I said? Do I need to ask that person—and God—to forgive me?

3. How can the group pray for those who use words to teach us and lead us from week to week (teachers, pastors, musicians, liturgists)?

4. How can my speech become more Christlike? Is there something specific the group can pray for (for example, my need to use words to witness, to be less critical, etc.)?

PRAYER TIME

PREPARATION

5-10 minutes

As you are comfortable, share any answers or parts of answers from questions 1-4. How would you like the group to pray for you between now and next time you meet?

Leader: Go around the circle, giving each person an opportunity to share his or her response to one or two of the reflection questions.

PRAYER

10-15 minutes

Spend a minute or two silently asking God to forgive you for hurting someone with your words or for being less than Christlike in your speech.

Spend some time using words (and songs) to praise God for who he is and what he has done.

Pray for the needs mentioned earlier by group members.

Close your prayer time by saying this prayer in unison:

Ask a group member to read these guidelines aloud before the prayer time begins. Feel free to substitute your own ideas for prayer, as you think best.

[Lord],

Hallowed be your name. . . .

Help us to really know you,
to bless, worship, and praise you
    for all your works
    and for all that shines forth from them:
        your almighty power, wisdom, kindness,
        justice, mercy, and truth. . . .

Help us to direct all our living—
    what we think, say, and do—
so that your name will never be blasphemed
    because of us
but always honored and praised. Amen.

—Answer 122 of the Heidelberg Catechism

PLANNING FOR MINISTRY

Leader: Discuss the "empty chair" strategy with your group. This implies a deliberate outward focus and a desire to grow. Is the group willing to commit to the strategy at this time?

Three more sessions remain in this course. Perhaps you want to talk with your group about any changes they'd like to make in the session format.

Regularly praying for someone is one of the most powerful and God-pleasing ways we can use our words. Are there persons for whom the entire group can pray this week?

If the group hasn't already done so, consider setting an empty chair in your circle at your next meeting. The chair can serve as a constant reminder of the next person God will bring into the group. Group members can pray for and actively seek persons to occupy that chair.

Session 5

RELATING WISELY

OPENING SHARE TIME

10-15 minutes

In today's passage, James bluntly tells God's people that they are an envious bunch, quarrelsome, full of selfish ambition, and devoted to things of this world. It's not a pretty picture.

Leader: Occasionally you may want to substitute your own opening share questions (or questions from your group) for ours.

1. Imagine a modern "James" looking into your denomination or congregation, then writing a letter expressing concern over some of its obvious faults. What might be some of the faults or weaknesses the letter mentions?
2. Now think about what James calls "humility that comes from wisdom." Who do you know (or who have you heard about) who exemplifies this trait? How does he or she show "humility"? Take a moment to tell the group about your choice.

BIBLE DISCOVERY TIME

20-30 minutes

Read James 3:13-16; 4:1-6. In this part of his letter, James describes some of the sinful tendencies he sees in the church's leaders and members—acts and attitudes that cause relationships between believers to disintegrate.

You may want to point out that, for now, we're skipping verses 17-18 of chapter 3; we'll pick up these verses later when we look at the medicine that James prescribes for the "bad news" he delivers in this section.

> [13]*Who is wise and understanding among you? Let him show it by his good life, by deeds done in the humility that comes from wisdom.* [14]*But if you harbor bitter envy and selfish ambition in your hearts, do not boast about it or deny the truth.* [15]*Such "wisdom" does not come down from heaven but is earthly, unspiritual, of the devil.* [16]*For where you have envy and selfish ambition, there you find disorder and every evil practice. . . .*

[1]What causes fights and quarrels among you? Don't they come from your desires that battle within you? [2]You want something but don't get it. You kill and covet, but you cannot have what you want. You quarrel and fight. You do not have, because you do not ask God. [3]When you ask, you do not receive, because you ask with wrong motives, that you may spend what you get on your pleasures.

[4]You adulterous people, don't you know that friendship with the world is hatred toward God? Anyone who chooses to be a friend of the world becomes an enemy of God. [5]Or do you think Scripture says without reason that the spirit he caused to live in us envies intensely? [6]But he gives us more grace. That is why Scripture says:

"God opposes the proud
but gives grace to the humble."

Leader: Refer to Helpful Notes when they pertain to your discussion.

Helpful Notes

- *Who is wise . . . among you?* James starts this section (3:1) by warning about the risks of being a teacher or leader in the church. He says these teachers vie for being considered wise, thereby showing themselves foolish. Of course, James's warnings apply to church members as well as teachers and church leaders. Especially in chapter 4, it's plain that he is addressing a broader audience.
- *You kill.* Theologians generally assume that James means this figuratively—looks and tongues can "kill."
- *Adulterous people.* James is accusing his readers of being unfaithful to God by becoming "friends of the world."
- *The spirit he caused to live in us envies intensely.* An alternate to the NIV translation is this: "He [God] yearns jealously after the spirit which he has made to dwell within us." God is a jealous God (Exod. 20:5). He demands that we be singularly devoted to him.

1. Skim the above passages and note the sinful attitudes and actions that indicate "sibling rivalry" between God's children. Which of these attitudes or actions do you see in the church at large today?

2. "What causes quarrels and fights among you?" James asks. Note how he answers his own question (4:1-4). How would you answer his question if it were applied to believers today?

3. James says we do not receive what we ask of God because we ask with our own selfish motives in mind. Give some examples of this kind of prayer.

4. What do you think: Are we less "worldly" than the believers James addresses? How do we know if we're becoming too friendly with the world? What are some of the warning signs?

Read James 3:17-18; 4:7-12. After the bad news comes the good news. Believers can stop the fighting, even the "desires that battle within" them. James tells us how.

Leader: Ask someone to read the introduction and the rest of today's Scripture aloud. Then discuss, using the questions that follow the passage.

17But the wisdom that comes from heaven is first of all pure; then peace-loving, considerate, submissive, full of mercy and good fruit, impartial and sincere.
18Peacemakers who sow in peace raise a harvest of righteousness.

7Submit yourselves, then, to God. Resist the devil, and he will flee from you. 8Come near to God and he will come near to you. Wash your hands, you sinners, and purify your hearts, you double-minded. 9Grieve, mourn and wail. Change your laughter to mourning and your joy to gloom. 10Humble yourselves before the Lord, and he will lift you up.

11Brothers, do not slander one another. Anyone who speaks against his brother or judges him speaks against the law and judges it. When you judge the law, you are not keeping it, but sitting in judgment on it. 12There is only one Lawgiver and Judge, the one who is able to save and destroy. But you—who are you to judge your neighbor?

Helpful Notes

- *Submit yourselves, then, to God.* In verses 7-10, James gives nine concrete actions that believers can take to overcome the problems he listed earlier. These actions are stated as commands, to be done immediately.
- *Wash your hands. . .purify your hearts.* The washing of hands symbolizes the external, doing the

right thing; purifying the heart symbolizes an internal, single-minded devotion to God.

- *Do not slander one another.* Avoiding slander and judgment follow naturally from being in right relationship with God (vv. 7-10). By slandering and judging each other, we violate our bond with the only true Judge.

1. How do you react to the idea of "humbling yourself"? May we be humble and still "assert ourselves"? How will our humility show in our relationships with others?

2. "Resist the devil, and he will flee from you," advises James. He depicts the devil as our adversary who uses our desires to lure us away from God and toward the things of this world. In practical terms, how can we go about "resisting the devil"?

3. "Come near to God and he will come near to you." In what ways can we come closer to God? What is your personal, preferred way to draw closer to God?

Leader: When discussing question 4, you might ask someone to read Ephesians 6:10-18 aloud. It suggests some ways that we can take a stand "against the devil's schemes."

4. "Humble yourselves before the Lord, and he will lift you up." Try getting at the meaning of this beautiful promise by rephrasing it in your own words. What does it mean to be "lifted up" by the Lord? When has this happened to you?

MAIN IDEAS

Ask someone to read Main Ideas aloud. Then read Good News in unison.

- Our selfish ambitions, envy, lack of humility, and addiction to worldly pleasures create rifts in our relationships with fellow believers.
- Such attitudes lead to fighting, slandering, and judging each other.
- God calls us to be peacemakers, to humble ourselves before God, and to devote ourselves to God and to Christlike living.

GOOD NEWS

We're not alone in our fight against our selfish ambitions and worldly desires. God will draw near and lift us up as we humble ourselves before him.

REFLECTION TIME

7-10 minutes

Jot down your personal reflections, using the questions and the space below.

Leader: You may want to remind the group of the A.C.T.S. format that patterns this time (adoration, confession, thanksgiving, supplication).

1. What have I learned about God today that makes me want to praise and thank him?

2. Did James remind me of something for which I need to ask God's forgiveness?

3. How can the group pray for me, as I try to "let go and let God"?

4. Is there something that's dividing and hurting our fellowship at church? in this group? How can the group pray about this?

PRAYER TIME

PREPARATION

5-10 minutes

Leader: As part of your preparation for prayer, you may want to read Isaiah 40:28-31. This beautiful passage offers renewed strength for those who hope in the Lord.

As you are comfortable, share any answers or parts of your answers from questions 1-4. Share especially those insights that will help the group to pray meaningfully with you and for you.

PRAYER

10-15 minutes

Ask a group member to read the guidelines aloud before the prayer time begins. An alternative to reading Answer 123 is to sing or read "Make Me a Channel of Your Peace," which sets to music the prayer of Francis of Assisi.

Begin with a minute of silence during which your group members may "humble themselves before the Lord." Silently thank and praise God for who he is and what he has done in your life. Or picture yourself bowing low before the Lord.

Pray for the needs mentioned earlier by group members. Supporting each other in honest, sincere prayer is one of the best ways of developing the bonds that God wants his children to have with each other.

Close your prayer time by saying the following prayer in unison.

[Lord],

Your kingdom come . . .

Rule us by your Word and Spirit in such a way
that more and more we submit to you.

Keep your church strong, and add to it.

Destroy the devil's work;
destroy every force which revolts against you
and every conspiracy against your Word.

Do this until your kingdom is so complete and perfect
that in it you are
all in all. Amen.

—Answer 123 of the Heidelberg Catechism

PLANNING FOR MINISTRY

Teachers and leaders in the church are in special need of our prayers and support. Perhaps each member of the group can call one leader or teacher during the week to thank him for the work he does and assuring him of the group's prayers.

Leader: If you try the suggested project, come with a list of names and phone numbers of church leaders and teachers.

Session 6

HANDLING OUR MONEY

OPENING SHARE TIME

10-15 minutes

1. Imagine you've inherited a million dollars from the proverbial distant aunt you hardly knew. Nobody knows you're suddenly rich. What would you do with your money? Mention at least a couple of things. Do you think that, in the long run, the money would be good for you?
2. Returning to the real world—do you ever think of yourself as "rich" in material possessions? If so, in comparison to whom?

Leader: Talking about our money and how we use it can be a touchy business. The first question should help the group get into the topic on a light note. Question 2 should provoke some thought about the relative wealth of North American Christians in a time of global poverty.

BIBLE DISCOVERY TIME

20-30 minutes

Read James 4:13-17. James has been urging Christians to be humble in all their ways. In this section of his letter, he extends the call to humility to wealthy (and arrogant) merchants, most of whom were probably from outside the Christian community. James reminds them—and us—who is really in control of everything.

Read the introduction aloud, noting how James addresses a somewhat different audience in this section (see Helpful Notes for more on this). Then read the passage to the group. Try to capture some of James's stern tone.

> *13 Now listen, you who say, "Today or tomorrow we*
> *will go to this or that city, spend a year there, carry on*
> *business and make money." 14 Why, you do not even*
> *know what will happen tomorrow. What is your life?*
> *You are a mist that appears for a little while and then*
> *vanishes. 15 Instead, you ought to say, "If it is the*
> *Lord's will, we will live and do this or that." 16 As it is,*
> *you boast and brag. All such boasting is evil.*
> *17 Anyone, then, who knows the good he ought to do*
> *and doesn't do it, sins.*

Helpful Notes

- *Now listen.* Literally, "Come now!" The phrase alerts readers that James is launching an attack, a serious indictment.
- *You who say.* James doesn't identify precisely who he is targeting here, but his description indicates that he is addressing merchants who

Refer to Helpful Notes when they pertain to your discussion. A group member may read them aloud.

carry on international trade by sea or caravan. Note that James does not call them brothers or even friends, but simply "you who say. . . ." That's evidence that most—if not all—of these merchants were from outside the Christian community.

Leader: James is not saying it's sinful for the merchants to engage in successful business practices. Rather, he is criticizing their self-confident arrogance, their assumption that they are in control of their lives.

1. What do you think these merchants are boasting and bragging about? What sinful assumptions are behind their boasting and their planning?
2. In the spirit of verse 15, Christians used to routinely close their announcements about their plans by adding "the Lord willing." Thus someone might say, "I'm going to visit Aunt Tillie in Toronto next week, the Lord willing." Do you still hear this expression (or its abbreviation, D.V.) used by Christians? Or has it largely dropped out of our vocabulary? Do you think we should say "the Lord willing" more often? Why or why not?
3. "What is your life?" asks James, adding that it is but "a mist that appears for a little while." What reaction does James intend this blunt statement to have on the merchants he's addressing? How do you as a believer react to it?

Ask someone to read the introductory comments and the passage. He or she may want to adopt an indignant tone for this section of James's letter.

Read James 5:1-6. In this section James addresses wealthy, *non-Christian* landowners who live in luxury and oppress the poor. As we read this stinging indictment, think about what it meant for the oppressed Christians to whom James wrote, and what it means for us today.

> *1 Now listen, you rich people, weep and wail because of the misery that is coming upon you. 2 Your wealth has rotted, and moths have eaten your clothes. 3 Your gold and silver are corroded. Their corrosion will testify against you and eat your flesh like fire. You have hoarded wealth in the last days. 4 Look! The wages you failed to pay the workmen who mowed your fields are crying out against you. The cries of the harvesters have reached the ears of the Lord Almighty. 5 You have lived on earth in luxury and self-indulgence. You have fattened yourselves in the day of slaughter. 6 You have condemned and murdered innocent men, who were not opposing you.*

Helpful Notes

- *Weep and wail.* Not out of repentance but "because of the misery that is coming upon you." It is not their riches that bring this judgment, but the way they've obtained and misused their wealth.
- *The Lord Almighty.* Our Father God is sovereign over all powers in heaven and on earth.
- *Fattened yourselves in the day of slaughter.* According to *The NIV Study Bible,* the "day of slaughter" refers to judgment day. "The wicked are like cattle that continue to fatten themselves on the very day they are to be slaughtered, totally unaware of coming destruction."

1. What sins of the rich, non-Christian landowners is James attacking in this section?

2. Imagine yourself a poor Christian, reading James's condemnation of the rich who oppressed you. What effect would this have on you?

3. In James's day, some Christians favored the rich (James 2:1-4), probably out of a desire to be like them or to gain their acceptance. Do you ever find yourself envying those who seem to have everything? Is James 5:1-6 a good antidote to those feelings? Why or why not?

4. Much like Abraham—who was called God's friend (James 2:23) and was very wealthy (Genesis 13:2)—North American Christians can be richly blessed with material well-being. We can praise God for his goodness. But what do we do with a passage like James 5:1-6? Are there some practical lessons here for us? What do you hear God telling you about your lifestyle in these verses?

Leader: Question 4 takes the group into sensitive and difficult areas. We can get very judgmental about our neighbor's "luxuries" and quite defensive about our own "necessities"! Steer clear of any talk that compares "my old Ford" with Joe's new BMW. Encourage, instead, some honest struggling with the question and some humble reflection. Ultimately, it's something each of us must answer for ourselves.

MAIN IDEAS

- As we live from day to day and make our plans for the future, we should not be arrogant. Rather, we should recognize that God is in control, and we are dependent on his favor.
- We should praise God for financial security and material well-being; yet we ought not to be charmed by wealth.

Ask someone to read Main Ideas aloud. Perhaps you can add some of the conclusions reached in question 4, above.

- If we extort from the poor or trample on others to gain our wealth, if we hoard our money or use it only for our own selfish pleasures, we won't survive God's judgment.
- The Lord Almighty hears and responds to the cries of the poor and oppressed. We should too.

GOOD NEWS

We can delight in God's material blessings! And we can show our gratitude by acting justly, loving mercy, and walking humbly with our God (Micah 6:8).

REFLECTION TIME

7-10 minutes

Leader: Group members work individually during Reflection Time.

Jot down your personal reflections, using the questions below.

1. What did I learn about God that moves me to praise him today?

2. Do I need to confess that money and possessions have been too important in my life?

3. Are there people I know who are unemployed and/or hard-pressed financially? For which oppressed peoples in our world should we pray?

4. How would I like a prayer partner to pray for me this week?

PRAYER TIME

PREPARATION

5-10 minutes

Please work through today's Preparation and Prayer with a partner. As you are comfortable, share any answers or parts of answers from questions 1-4.

Move right into the prayer time with your partner(s).

Leader: The partnership approach is for variation; it will also help each person become involved. Encourage group members to choose someone other than their spouse for their prayer partner. It's OK to have some groups of three. Include yourself in one of the groups.

PRAYER

5-10 minutes

Partners may pray aloud for each other, based on their conversation earlier.

At the end of your prayer, join together in a single large group. Close your prayer time by saying this prayer in unison:

Note the reduced time for prayer this week. After the partners have prayed for and with each other (about five minutes), call the group back together. Lead them in saying the closing prayer in unison.

[Dear Lord],

Give us today our daily bread. . . .

Do take care of all our physical needs
so that we come to know
  that you are the only source of everything good,
  and that neither our work and worry
  nor your gifts
  can do us any good without your blessing.

And help us to give up our trust in creatures
and to put trust in you alone. Amen.

—Answer 125 of the Heidelberg Catechism

PLANNING FOR MINISTRY

Next week is our final session on the book of James. Today you may want to talk about what material the group wants to study next.

Is the group doing all it can to pray for new members? Pray that newcomers will be encouraged to join as you plan to start new study material in the next few weeks.

Session 7

WAITING PATIENTLY AND PRAYERFULLY

OPENING SHARE TIME

10-15 minutes

"Life in the fast lane" is the way some people describe our "hurry-up" society. We want fast food and fast service. Even the mail isn't fast enough—some of us who use e-mail refer to regular mail as "snail mail." We tend to be an impatient bunch!

1. Mention some other things that show the fast pace of life today.
2. To what extent has this fast pace affected your own degree of patience?

Leader: For an alternate question, ask, "When have you had to wait patiently or persevere through a time of suffering or other difficulty? What did you learn from your experience?"

BIBLE DISCOVERY TIME

20-30 minutes

Read James 5:7-12. James has just challenged and comforted the believers with the assurance that the Lord will justly condemn the rich who victimize them. Now he returns to the advice with which he began his letter: be patient in the face of suffering. Trust in God. Endure. Persevere. And, as always, watch your words.

> *[7]Be patient, then, brothers, until the Lord's coming. See how the farmer waits for the land to yield its valuable crop and how patient he is for the autumn and spring rains. [8]You too, be patient and stand firm, because the Lord's coming is near. [9]Don't grumble against each other, brothers, or you will be judged. The Judge is standing at the door!*
>
> *[10]Brothers, as an example of patience in the face of suffering, take the prophets who spoke in the name of the Lord. [11]As you know, we consider blessed those who have persevered. You have heard of Job's perseverance and have seen what the Lord finally brought about. The Lord is full of compassion and mercy.*

Ask one or two group members to read the introductory comments and the Bible passage. As you lead the group in discussing the questions, you may want to refer to several verses in chapter 1 that also deal with patience and self-control (see James l:4-5, 19-20, 26).

[12]Above all, my brothers, do not swear—not by heaven or by earth or by anything else. Let your "Yes" be yes, and your "No," no, or you will be condemned.

Leader: Refer to Helpful Notes when they pertain to your discussion. You may want to ask a group member to read these notes aloud.

Helpful Notes

- *See how the farmer waits.* The farmer cannot bring the rains—God alone can do that—so he must wait patiently. In the same way, we must wait for God to bring about our salvation; only he can do that. The farmer also waits patiently because he trusts that the harvest will come. In the same way, we can trust that the Lord will return to make things right.
- *You . . . have seen what the Lord finally brought about.* The reference here is not to Christ's sacrifice on the cross but to Job's eventual restoration.
- *Do not swear.* James's theme of caution in speech returns here. Swearing by God's name that something is true or untrue is misusing God's name. In good Jewish fashion, James considers the breaking of the third commandment the worst sin imaginable.

1. "Be patient. Stand firm." This is good advice for people enduring persecution and eagerly waiting for the Lord to return and set things straight. But how does James's advice to apply to our situation today?

When discussing question 2, you may want to read or refer to the Parable of the Ten Virgins (Matt. 25:1-13). Christ concludes this parable with this warning: "Therefore keep watch, because you do not know the day or the hour."

2. We know that our Lord will return. But do we have the same sense of urgency about this as the Christians whom James addressed? Should we? What should be our attitude toward Christ's return?
3. Read verse 12 once more. Is James condemning all use of oaths? What does the verse say about honoring a commitment, a promise, or one's signature on a contract? Does it say anything about today's proliferating lawsuits?

Read James 5:13-20. James ends his letter by reminding his readers that in bad times and good, in sickness and in health, the prayer of faith is "powerful and effective." Pray for each other, says James, and be ready to help those who wander from the path of truth.

[13]Is any one of you in trouble? He should pray. Is anyone happy? Let him sing songs of praise. [14]Is any one

of you sick? He should call the elders of the church to pray over him and anoint him with oil in the name of the Lord. [15]*And the prayer offered in faith will make the sick person well; the Lord will raise him up. If he has sinned, he will be forgiven.* [16]*Therefore confess your sins to each other and pray for each other so that you may be healed. The prayer of a righteous man is powerful and effective.*

[17]*Elijah was a man just like us. He prayed earnestly that it would not rain, and it did not rain on the land for three and a half years.* [18]*Again he prayed, and the heavens gave rain, and the earth produced its crops.*

[19]*My brothers, if one of you should wander from the truth and someone should bring him back,* [20]*remember this: Whoever turns a sinner from the errors of his way will save him from death and cover over a multitude of sins.*

Helpful Notes

- *Elders.* Refers to those holding the office of elder, not necessarily senior citizens.
- *Anoint him with oil.* The verses about anointing a sick person with oil (then widely regarded as a curative) have been hotly debated. The Roman Catholic Church finds here one of its sacraments for dying, administered by a priest when a believer's death is imminent. Faith healers and those in the "signs and wonders" movement have also appealed to these verses. Of course, when oil is used to anoint a sick person, the oil itself cannot cure—only God can. This act is done in God's name and must therefore be accompanied by prayer.
- *Will make the sick person well.* James is not saying that healing will *always* happen. If this were the case, believers would never have to die. Rather, James is providing a general rule of thumb: the Christian community must assume the responsibility of providing means of healing and prayer to those who need it.

1. Some Christians today practice anointing the sick with oil, then praying for their healing. What do you think about this? Should the church encourage it? Why or why not?

2. Have you personally witnessed or experienced the healing power of prayer? Can you share your experience?

3. Prayer is powerful and effective, says James (5:16). If you had to explain this to a nonbeliever, what would you say?

4. When is it easier for you to pray—when things are going well or when you're in difficulty of some kind? Why?

Leader: When discussing question 5, you may want to explore whether James's advice to "confess your sins to each other" is general advice or if it's tied to healing situations (v. 15).

5. Some believers find that confessing their sins to a brother or sister in Christ is edifying. They feel a need to unburden themselves to a fellow human being. What do you think about this? Should we confess our sins to each other more often than we do?

MAIN IDEAS

Consider having the group give their own summary of Main Ideas and Good News, then compare theirs with those we've supplied.

- Be patient when suffering. Persevere. The Lord is coming soon!
- Don't use your words to pick on each other or blaspheme God. Instead, pull together as a community and support each other by what you say (5:9, 12-13, 16) and do (5:14, 19).
- Pray in every situation. Pray for each other, especially during illness. Prayer is powerful and effective.
- Help those who wander from the faith.

GOOD NEWS

We await a new heaven and a new earth when there will be no more death or mourning or crying or pain, for the old order of things will have passed away (Rev. 21:4).

REFLECTION TIME

7-10 minutes

Because there is only one question to answer, you may want to spend less than the allotted time. Ask group members to jot down requests that they are willing to share with the others in the group.

James has urged us to pray earnestly for each other. To help the group do that, please focus on just one question: How would I like the group to pray for me today?

You may want to ask for prayers for patience to endure a difficult situation you're experiencing. Or maybe you'd like the group to pray that your faith will be strengthened in some specific way. You know your needs. Please let the group support you in prayer. You may use the space below to jot things down, if you wish.

PRAYER TIME

PREPARATION

5-10 minutes

Please tell the group how you would like them to pray for you today.

Leader: You may want to jot down (on a sheet of newsprint) the personal needs the group members mention. Consult the sheet during the prayer time.

PRAYER

10-15 minutes

You may want to begin your prayer time by singing a song that asks God to hear your prayer—for example, "Hear Our Prayer, O Lord," or "Lord, Listen to Your Children Praying."

Ask a group member to read the guidelines before your prayer time begins. To set up for the prayer time, place an empty chair in the middle of the room. Ask the group to stand in a circle around the chair.

Each person is invited to sit in the center of the circle (one at a time!). The others stand, place their hands on that person, and pray for him or her. The prayers may include and go beyond needs the person has requested. Thanks for the person and his or her presence in the group is also appropriate.

Close with a favorite song of praise (a few examples: "He Has Done Great Things," "Praise God from Whom All Blessings Flow," "God Is So Good," "Great Is Thy Faithfulness"). Or, if you prefer, read a praise Psalm (such as Psalm 103) responsively.

PLANNING FOR MINISTRY

Leader: We encourage you to send your reactions to this material to

Acts 2/Faith On-line
CRC Publications
2850 Kalamazoo Ave. SE
Grand Rapids, MI 49560

Thank you!

James suggests that we pray for those who are sick. Make a list of such persons for whom the group would like to pray during the week. If many names are mentioned, divide them between group members. Another possibility would be for the entire group to visit someone who is ill and pray with and for that person.

You may also want to review the group goals you made at the beginning and note any progress you have made. Have you decided what you are going to study next? Will you change location, schedule of meetings, or format?

Please take time to evaluate this *Acts 2* course. Doing so will benefit your own group and will help CRC Publications make improvements that will benefit many other groups like yours. Here are a few questions to consider as a group: Is the Opening Share Time effective? Do the Bible Discovery questions produce good discussion? Have the Reflection Time and Prayer Time become a meaningful part of your meetings? Has Planning for Ministry become part of your group process?

Revisit your plans to invite new people. The beginning of a new study is an excellent time to invite others to your group.

APPENDIX A

GROUP GOALS PLANNING SHEET

1. We plan for our group to grow and to spawn a new group by ______________________
____.

   How are we doing?

2. We plan to have an empty chair at every meeting and to pray for a person(s) to come and fill that chair. _____yes _____no

   How are we doing?

3. We plan to pray three or four times a week for each of the _____ unchurched persons we have identified.

   How are we doing?

4. We plan to invite, on an average, _____ new people each month.

   How are we doing?

5. We plan to sponsor _____ social events this year.

   How are we doing?

6. We plan to do _____ service projects this year.

   How are we doing?

7. Additional group goals:

   Special joys:

   Problem areas:

Other titles in the Acts 2 Series:

Spiritual Aerobics

Building the Body

Caring Connections

Lightening the Load